Smarty-Pants: How to Become a Valedictorian

Ellen Parry Lewis

Metal Lunchbox Publishing

Copyright © 2018 Ellen Parry Lewis
Illustrations and Design © 2018 SF Varney
All rights reserved.
ISBN: 0-9843437-5-X
ISBN-13: 978-0-9843437-5-1

DEDICATION

To my wonderful parents, who always encouraged me to simply try my best.

CONTENTS

1	Winning the Game	1
2	Do Your Best	Pg #5
3	When an A+ Isn't Good Enough	Pg #11
4	Know Your Teachers	Pg #17
5	Know Your Classmates	Pg #23
6	Get Social	Pg #27
7	Skirt Made Out of Wallpaper	Pg #33
8	Where Are We Now?	Pg #37

Acknowledgements

Author Bio

Winning the game

Not to sound like a complete show-off, but I'm smart. I know I am. I'm not talking super genius, college-graduate-at-age-ten smart, but my IQ is certainly well above average. So, it's not far-fetched to believe that I was the 2006 valedictorian at my high school out of about 350 seniors.

And yet, I certainly wasn't the only smart kid walking around the halls of my high school. As a matter of fact, I remember various teachers and parents playfully teasing, "What was in the water the year your class was born?" Not only were many of us "smart," but we were highly competitive, self-motivated kids who not only wanted to jump over obstacles, but obliterate them.

Now many people would over-simplify who becomes the valedictorian by saying it's whoever is the smartest in the grade. Yes, smarts have something to do with it. But we all know people who are incredibly smart, and yet they flunk all of their tests. We also know people who get straight A's who maybe aren't the sharpest. So, there's clearly more to it than that. Out of the hundreds of kids in my high school, I find it extremely possible that I didn't boast the highest IQ, and yet I was the one who claimed the title of valedictorian.

Perseverance. That's a huge part of what it came down to ultimately. There are of course other contributing factors, but the valedictorian is the one who doesn't get tired of trying their best, of being their best.

My uncle, Dan Rozinski, was the valedictorian of Lenape Regional High School in New Jersey in 1980. He once told me that becoming the valedictorian was about having the desire and ability to conquer the material given to you.

"Being intelligent sure helps, but it's not the only attribute necessary," said Mark Schoonover, who graduated tenth out of 300-some students at Winslow Township High School in New Jersey in 2005. "You also need to be diligent, engaged, and unwilling to settle for coasting."

A friend of mine in high school, Emily DiLorenzo, who graduated sixth in our class, said, "When it comes down to it, I think the person who ends up number one is there because they had the extra drive and competitive nature to get there."

The need to persevere. The desire to conquer. Unwilling to settle. The extra drive. Perhaps these sound a bit hyperbolic; after all, it's just high school. But I still got a kick out of approaching the road to the valedictorian title as a quest of sorts, a strategic war.

While I was still in high school, I remember my mom driving me somewhere, good-naturedly laughing at how high my grades were that marking period. She jokingly asked what my secret was. "School is just a game," I replied. "And it's the people who figure out the rules to the game who can ultimately win it." Years later, I'm sticking with that assessment.

And this game analogy is common among those who graduate at or near the top of their class.

"School is a game. There's a strategy you can use," Gina Coyle said, who graduated in the top ten of her class from my high school a couple of years ahead of me. Her one regret? "I found out freshman year I was in the top ten. I wish I knew my grades from all four years went toward my class rank from the very beginning. It wasn't even on my radar, so I didn't know my grades all the way back from freshman year even counted! I probably would have finished higher if I had been playing the game the whole time."

Sandy Hogg, who graduated in the top five the year after I did, said that being the valedictorian is "a measure of your ability to master the system, especially in terms of how GPA is recognized."

Now, there are people out there who find that becoming valedictorian falls into their lap. (Lucky ducks.) "I just took all of the honors classes because the other classes were too easy for me," Dan told me.

But if you come from a large high school or have a competitive class, there are helpful tricks to be learned—little-known rules for *winning the game*. So get in touch with your competitive side, and dive in.

Do Your Best

There are many tricks to be utilized in giving yourself an advantage—small maneuvers to outpace your fellow competitors. Though pure, solid academic footing is the foundation for becoming a valedictorian.

It's always helpful when you've had the desire to learn instilled in you as a young child from your parents or family members.

"I learned to read very early, really before I went to school….My mother read to me every single day," recalled

Virginia Parrish, a long-time teacher who graduated third from her own high school class in 1966.

She said her parents tried their best to make learning hands-on, saying how her father not only explained how an eclipse worked, but *showed* her by using a light bulb.

Remembered childhood experiences can also have a huge impact on retaining a lifelong love of learning. "We read every roadside history marker in Pennsylvania, New Jersey, and Delaware," Virginia said, laughing at the childhood memories.

However, regardless of your own childhood, keeping that curiosity and thirst for knowledge makes the journey to the top of your class that much more fulfilling.

Ultimately, you need to determine your own learning style. Virginia found that pneumonic devices and a good memory were her primary tools.

I also found that using my excellent memory was helpful in learning and obtaining top grades. Sometimes before an essay or short answer test, a teacher would give us the questions ahead of time. When this happened, I didn't just read and study the material—I wrote down the answers exactly as I would as if it were the real test. I then studied and read those answers, so that I had them nearly memorized and ready to regurgitate come test time. Being prepared is never a waste of time.

A common complaint I've noticed with English teachers especially is that students will write a research paper and then click print without glancing at it ever again. Simple steps such as reading and editing your work before submitting it will ensure that you dont make manny mistaks.

So make those practice flash cards, stretch your memory to its limits, participate in class.

Do the homework.

"I always did every bit of work, just because I figured if the teacher assigned the work, it should be done," Dan Rozinski told me.

Joe Boales graduated fourth from his Kingsway Regional High School class of about 350 students in 2008. Kingsway is found in Woolwich Township, New Jersey. "Planning your homework around extra-curriculars can be difficult, especially with intense course loads. There were certainly times that I stayed up until 4 a.m. because I had to work at my part-time job and had homework in every class. Normally, a lot of those assignments are assigned on a regular schedule, like weekly, but sometimes they're all assigned on the same day and due the next day. That's where determination comes in—getting it all done and not giving up," Joe told me.

Staying up until 4 a.m. might work for students like Joe (and was the way I myself would handle the extreme workload some nights). But knowing yourself and how you work best is also part of being able to do the work and do it well.

"Being the valedictorian or doing well doesn't always mean doing everything perfectly. It's about managing your energy—understanding what you need to do right and where your energy needs to be focused," Sandy Hogg said. This might mean learning what you can "get away with." Is attendance considered when your grade is calculated? Can you drop the lowest test score? If you can drop that lowest score, "do yourself a favor, get some sleep, and move on," Sandy said, preferring a good night's rest to an all-nighter spent studying.

"I would often do my homework in the morning because my brain was fresh," Sandy went on to explain. "I would rather go to bed at eleven and wake up at four or five than keep working straight into the early hours of the morning. It's about knowing yourself and when you're the most productive."

Do the extra credit. Unless you already have a one hundred in a class and the extra credit is only to boost that final grade, it's almost always a good bet. Even the difference between a 99 in a class and a 100 can make a difference when class standings can be separated by fractions of points.

I spoke with high school senior Nina Lopergolo from Highland Regional High School in New Jersey in April of 2017. She was set to graduate as one of several tied valedictorians from her school out of more than 300 students in her graduating class. She recalled a particularly humorous extra credit assignment in which she participated. "One time for extra credit, my psychology teacher made us walk around school *all day* with these paper brain hats on our heads. Of course I did it because I wanted the extra credit. And the looks I got from the other students in the halls were pretty awesome too."

The brain hat — More brain hat

Sometimes doing "extra" can also be just as effective as doing official extra credit. "I'd always take advantage of extra credit opportunities, but I'd also go the extra mile to make my work the best in general," Laura Oliveto said. Laura was the valedictorian of my alma mater, Williamstown High School, in 2015. She graduated with 419 students. "I guess I tried to set myself up so that there was no way I could get less than an A on anything. I remember for my one government project, the class was split into two 'parties,' and we ran against each other in an election. My group went above and beyond; we made shirts, hats, personalized giveaways, a giant trifold, you name it. Needless to say, we won, but it definitely helped that we did so much extra. Plus I think being competitive helps too; I looked at everything as a competition that I wanted to win."

Finally, there's one other traditional tactic that I myself used. I was occasionally tutored. Even though I was a straight-A student, not every single subject came easily to me—namely chemistry and geometry. Fortunately, my uncle was and is a chemical engineer, and I leaned strongly on his expertise and good teaching skills during the year I took chemistry. When I struggled occasionally with math, I sought help with various people, including older students who lived nearby and still knew the material well.

I mentioned high school senior Nina Lopergolo. As you can imagine, her academic resume is packed with straight A's in honors and AP courses. However, one day she received that most detestable of sights to an academic overachiever—a B in her physics class! And so, she swallowed her pride and immediately sought the help of a tutor. "I never needed that kind of help before, so it was kind of hard to admit that I needed someone else's help. It was embarrassing and awkward, but afterwards I was so happy because I don't know how I would have survived that class without him," she said of her tutor. After seeking help from this tutor, she found that she was receiving exceptionally high marks, far surpassing other students in her class.

Also, don't discount just asking your teachers for help, though always make sure you're in their good graces. Emily Severance, an English teacher at Timber Creek Regional High School in New Jersey and an academic overachiever in her own time suggested, "Do all of your work. If a teacher sees you trying and you're struggling, they are more likely to give you extra help or time or chances when you need them."

As Nina always tried her best, this benevolent attitude from her teachers came in very helpful a couple of times during her high school career. "I was obviously very open about my aspirations," she said. "I worked hard constantly, not just when it was crunch time." And so when she found herself missing the mark just slightly, she said a couple of her teachers were more willing "to look the other way and throw those points" to her in some way.

Nevertheless, if you're on the journey to academic perfection, don't wait until you and your grade are truly struggling to seek help. If my grade was reaching the lower regions of an A, I got help right away! It's easier to stop a grade from falling proactively than to try to pull a low one up to where you want it. And so even if you're the "smart kid," don't be afraid to ask for help! (And chances are, if you're already doing great in the class by other people's standards, catching you up to speed won't take much time in the first place.)

Now I just used the term "academic perfection." Obviously, no one is perfect, and as a result, your schoolwork can't always be perfect either. Sometimes you mess up, and the consequences are unavoidable. Other times, I found that drastic measures prevented me from receiving a bad grade:

Me: <*On a payphone during lunch.* Side note: Yes, oddly enough, those still existed while I was in school as cell phones were strictly banned.> Mom, can you be here to pick me up from school in the next 45 minutes?

My Wonderful, Supportive, Beautiful Mother: Sure, what's wrong?

Me: I completely forgot about a homework assignment I was supposed to do for my English class!

My Mom: Okay. I'll be there soon.

    This scenario only happened a couple times during my entire high school career, though it was nice having the luxury to skip out so that I didn't receive a zero for a homework assignment.
    When I told my uncle, Dan, what I did, he laughed. "Well, you certainly took that to an extreme." When that happened to him, he said he took the opportunity to talk to the teacher one-on-one. "Look, you know I *never* forget homework assignments," he would say. "I would negotiate to get the extra time." And for a good student, it's certainly easier to make an exception.
    Yes, I suppose I took the drastic approach as it was especially cautious and not dependent on my teacher's goodwill. That being said, I had the luxury to take that extreme cautionary measure since my mom was at home during the day. If that's not an option for you or you are confident in the good rapport you have with a teacher, Dan's approach was completely effective, and arguably more respectable.
    I cannot overemphasize the importance of achieving good grades through consistent hard work and good study habits. But sometimes these simple, straight-forward acts are not enough. Sometimes, the strategies toward winning the game go deeper than that. So....

When an A+ Isn't Good Enough

Different schools calculate GPAs differently.
    Some systems of calculating GPAs are straight forward. Example: Getting an A means you have, well, you know, an A.
    Other systems are a bit more complicated. Example: Take the grade you earned in a class. Divide that grade by the number of students in your class and add that resultant number to π. Take *that* number and multiply it to the amount of times you tripped going up the stairs in your high school, spilling your books and

belongings all over the floor like a doofus. (Side note: Under this system, my GPA is approximately a 21.42. Do the math.)

My particular high school used a weighted GPA system out of 100% as opposed to a 4.0. A 100% in a college prep (CP) class earned you a 100%. Honors classes added 8 points to your final marking period grade, and advanced placement (AP) classes earned you 15 points added to your final marking period grade.

As an eighth grade student preparing to go to high school, several teachers and guidance counselors gave all of us students these words of advice: "In classes that you feel confident in, challenge yourself! Take those honors classes! However, don't take *all* honors classes, or you may end up a stressed-out mess, closer to brain-craving zombies than actual human beings. Your grades will suffer as a result, and you will end up living in a trash can." (Note: Not *actual* words of anyone, but you get the gist.)

And so, like other kids in my grade, I was prepared to take all honors classes except for one CP history class my freshman year of high school.

And that's when a fateful trip to my dentist changed everything:

My dentist: You're a smart kid. If anyone can handle all honors classes, it's you. Go for it!

Me: Abe Ooo Rah! (Translation: "Maybe you're right!" I mean, I had dental tools in my mouth.)

And so I switched that last CP class to an honors class, and I was so happy I did. Especially since I noticed the least difficulty difference between honors and CP classes in our school's history department.

I got straight A's that year, and every year after that as I kept all honors classes and began to add AP classes to my schedules as well. (Admission: Final exam grades counted as an entire fifth marking period grade at my school. And I got a B on a final exam *once* in a typing class. Apparently I didn't know how to properly indent a business letter....)

Mark Schoonover had a similar experience with being discouraged from taking too many difficult classes, but he relied on his own self-awareness rather than his dentist to make the final decision. "My first strategy was to remember that guidance counselors don't really know what you're capable of. If you want to take five AP classes your senior year, do it. My guidance counselor told me it'd be too much. I did it anyway, and had the best year grade-wise of my high school career. I think it was because I was engaged, challenged."

Once you know exactly how your school calculates GPAs, you'll be able to best assess how you can achieve the highest one possible. I knew that I was able to get all A's, and even straight 100s for one marking period during my senior year, in all honors and AP classes. However, I knew that if I ever felt the burden of too much work and not enough time in a day, I was prepared with my fallback college prep course—English. Now, I'm a writer. I love English, and it comes easy to me. I noticed, though, that in my high school, the difference between an honors English class and a college prep English class was usually extreme. I'm fairly certain the college prep classes read one picture book each marking period while the honors classes read a new classic novel every week. (An obvious exaggeration, though not as extreme as you might think in regards to the honors classes.) And so, since I almost never struggled in a class, English would be an easy choice if I needed to give myself a breather. I never did need that workload reduction, thankfully. But keep in mind that in many schools it would be better to get an A in a college prep class than a C in an honors class.

Additionally, as I already mentioned, there seemed to be very little difference between my school's honors history and college prep history classes. And so, even if I had found myself to be struggling in that class, I knew that dropping to a college prep class would not be an option for me because, quite frankly, it wouldn't help.

Now if you're the kind of person who can handle all honors and AP coursework, try your best to give yourself a head start on your classmates. Nina Lopergolo said that she was fast-tracked in middle school. Many districts have programs like these, allowing you to take advanced mathematics or science before you even enter high school so that you can essentially skip a grade in those subjects. Sometimes, this means that you can get an opportunity to take an AP class before other students who might only have honors or CP classes open to them in a lower science or math subject.

"Choosing classes is important," Joe Boales agreed. "If you're planning to take all of the AP classes, you also need to start early. Some AP classes have prerequisites."

If you weren't fast-tracked, but know yourself to be fully capable of this, look into whether your district has any tests you could take, allowing you to pass out of a certain subject and arrive at those upper-classmen AP classes sooner. Sometimes, a simple phone call is all it could take to place you in those harder classes, even if you did poorly on an initial placement test.

Knowing your personal limits and constructively challenging yourself is one thing, but you should also endeavor to know your particular class. As I already said, my specific graduating class was made up of super-intelligent mutants. And so a minor lapse on my part could have resulted in a greatly decreased class rank. However, not all classes are like that. Gina Coyle told me, "I realized I was better off if I took a mix of college prep and honors courses....I believe in working smarter, not harder." She knew that her A's in college prep courses would easily compete with the B's of some of her honors class counterparts. And so she surprised people when she easily came out in the top ten of her class. "I was able to kind of fly under the radar. People said, 'Why's she so high up? She doesn't even take all honors classes.' "

Now, sometimes you have to achieve A's in all honors and AP classes in order to remain competitive. But usually you can't truly take *all* honors and AP classes.

Each year, I had to take a science with a lab two days a week. This left an awkward three-day-a-week gap for an elective course. Three-day electives were few and far between, but choir was an option, and as I always enjoyed singing, I took that. However, after my freshman year, I realized something horrible—I was receiving a 100% in choir! "Isn't that good?" you might ask. Yes, usually a 100% is phenomenal. Except choir wasn't an honors course. In fact, there was no such thing as an honors elective, especially a three-day elective. And as my GPA was over 100% due to my weighted classes, a 100% in choir was actually *lowering* my GPA! Now, I wasn't the only one taking three-day choir. A lot of us were. And that realization is just what I needed to give myself the advantage.

I dropped choir and switched to a three-day-a-week study hall.

A lot of students find study halls helpful in getting all of their work done. "I made sure to take a study hall, at least a three-day-a-week study hall with lab science the other two. This way, I had extra time to get work done since I was involved in so many clubs and sports," Emily Severance said.

I took a study hall in order to ponder life's great questions, write awe-inspiring papers, and change the face of academia. And thus, I would pass notes on extremely important topics to my friend, Emily DiLorenzo, such as the following copy of a real note from study hall:

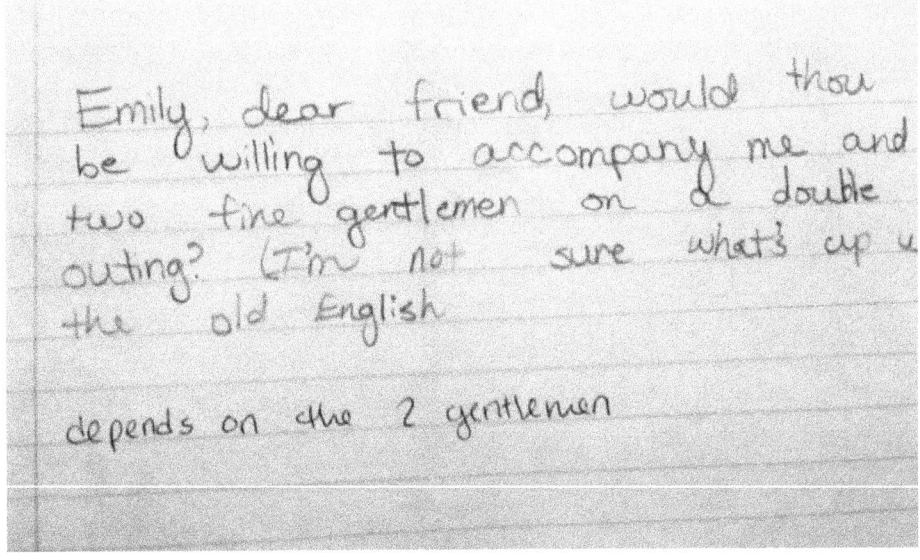

First of all, I have no idea what she was so hesitant about. We had a delightful time. But more to the point, I didn't take study hall in order to work myself to the bone. In actuality, I used it as a time to decompress. And yet, taking this study hall actually *improved* my GPA! You see, I couldn't receive a grade for a study hall, and so my GPA was calculated with one less class than the others' who took an actual elective. Therefore, I could actually get ahead of the game by writing silly notes and making plans to go on double dates.

Now, I didn't allow myself to become a GPA robot. I still did take one elective each year that lowered my GPA—acting or musical theater. Honestly, this was something I loved. Also, all of the other top kids were taking an elective like this, and so my one study hall was enough to help put me over the edge without compromising on my theater classes, which goes back to knowing your classmates and knowing what you can personally handle. And I was glad for this GPA-lowering break in my day. I got to perform Broadway songs and dance in exciting dance numbers. I learned that I can't shimmy to save my life. I once had the opportunity to be the Wicked Witch of the West in a play for young children. (I absolutely loved the chance to be the "bad guy," as I was usually typecast as "the mom.") I was once a sheep who was also a judge in a court case against Mary (the one who had a little lamb). My family still talks about that silly sheep role and how it almost made everyone pee their pants laughing.

So I was able to give myself a fun break and settle for a 100%.

Know Your Teachers

Just like there are all kinds of students, there are all kinds of teachers. (Obviously.) But learning to deal with these different kinds of teachers is a huge part of strategizing so that you can achieve good grades and ultimately win the game.

    I considered each teacher as an individual, completely separate even from the subject they taught. As early as possible in a new class, study your teacher! Learn what they like and don't like. To what do they seem to respond positively? Do they like a bit of healthy class chaos or do they cringe if someone sneezes? Do they like it when students seem to grasp the material they're teaching easily? Or do they want you to work for that A with the same difficulty that a person climbing a mountain in ice skates might experience?

I once had a teacher who prided himself on his class being incredibly difficult. A's were not given in his class—they were *earned*. He even gave out pencils to mark the rarely received A, and yes, sadly, I still have mine:

Another teacher I had very frequently showed us movies "related" to the class. (I'm still not sure that crime solving television shows were entirely related to our science class, but far be it from my high school self to complain about a little down time in the middle of a busy day.)

Once you've figured out what kind of a person your teacher is and what they want out of their students, just give them what they want!

My freshman year, I had a teacher who announced on the first day that it was her very first year teaching. As a result, the students in my class proceeded to eat her alive all year. (No, not literally.) I figured she could probably really use a student who simply sat quietly and actually listened in her class. And so that's what I set out to be. I got straight A's.

For the teachers who wanted to be the most difficult teachers on the planet, I played up the times when I struggled with anything. I let them know that I was having a hard time, sought their expertise, and thus hopefully gave their egos the needed boost. (Side note: Obviously not all difficult teachers are on a power trip, though they usually still appreciate you looking for help if you're struggling.) If you're not struggling in the difficult teacher's class, try your best to come up with *something* that you're not completely clear on. Don't lie—teachers are smart and can often see through a complete act, but certainly highlight your moments of weakness to these teachers, however rare. I did this for my difficult teachers, and I got—I'm sorry, *earned*—straight A's.

Some teachers like the goofy kid, so I played up my quirky side. I got straight A's.

Some like the star pupil. (That was an easy aspect to highlight for me!) I got straight A's.

Some teachers, believe it or not, like the dumb kid. So, much like the difficult teachers, I showed them every time I didn't get something 100%. Then...I got straight A's.

Frank Broomell graduated in 2005 in the top ten from St. Augustine, a boys' school with 106 students in his graduating class. He believed that knowing your teacher was important even when it came to studying for tests. "I think part of it is just trying to get a feeling for what each teacher is looking for. They each have their own styles and approaches. One teacher might be very focused on wanting to know the details of how many people fought at a specific battle in the Civil War, for example. So you need to focus a lot on those aspects. A different teacher might be less focused on details and more focused on what an event represents as a change or a shift. What did x mean for the United States at that point in time?" And so he found that using preliminary tests as examples for how to approach a specific teacher and their exams in the future helped him throughout his high school career. "It helps you save yourself from spinning your wheels on things that ultimately won't end up on the test."

Gina Coyle took a straight-forward approach to dealing with her teachers. "Just give the teacher what they want and you're going to be successful." She recalled having a unique writing teacher. "It's almost like she wanted to write your paper." And so

Gina would write her papers early, approach the teacher after class, and say, "Here's my draft. Do you want to read it over?" Even if she offered advice that was completely different from something Gina would usually do on her own, Gina "just wrote down what she said and turned it in." Good grades ensued.

(As an added bonus, Gina's story is a good lesson in not procrastinating! "Do your work early. It gives you more time to find out what your teachers want.")

My good friend, Jessica Mumford, had a very unique experience in her high school, where she graduated in the top ten before graduating as the valedictorian from her community college and then graduating magna cum laude from Rowan University. At her high school, she had a teacher with a very unique, unwritten demand—join the drama club, of which she was the adviser. "Before she was my teacher, I had heard from the other students in my class that you needed to join the drama club if you wanted an A. I thought, oh really? And then I got a B my first marking period, but right on the edge of an A. I thought maybe it was just a fluke, especially since English was always my strongest subject, and that I just had to get used to my teacher and her style of teaching. But then I got another high B the second marking period." Changing nothing about her work ethic as she was already trying her best, she decided to actually give this unusual advice a try, and she joined the drama club. That being said, Jessica didn't compromise who she was in the process. "I'm not an actress by any stretch of the imagination, but I am an artist. So I joined the school play in order to do set design for them. I also needed extra-curricular activities for my college applications, so it kind of killed two birds with one stone." She got straight A's in her class after that. "And interestingly enough, I was in two of her classes that year, and I started getting A's in both of them. Once I was in, I was in. And as silly as it sounds, I truly believed that that was the reason for my success in that teacher's classes."

Unfortunately for this teacher, she did encounter an unusual problem during Jessica's year in her class. "Well, the other students basically tried to stage a coup of sorts," Jessica said, laughing at the bizarre memory. A vast majority of the students decided that she was an unfair teacher, and chose to rise up in a sort of rebellion. They all stood up and declared that they would not listen to her or accept her classroom expectations. "There were only a few of us not standing with them. They kept telling us, 'Come on. Solidarity. We all need to be in this together.' I told them, 'Sorry guys, I really need a good grade for college scholarships.'"

They can't punish all of us, some students will say. Yes. Yes, they can. But Jessica was not punished, went on to receive a high grade from that teacher, and ultimately a high class rank upon graduation. "All of the other students who did that were sent to the office, and I'm pretty sure they all did really bad in the class."

Oddly enough, the situation that Jessica described is not the first time I've heard of such a thing. My advice? If your teacher is engaged in something truly unfair or unethical, go to your school's administration about your concerns. But trying a civil disobedience tactic in the classroom where your teacher is essentially your dictator is almost never a good idea.

Randy Ford also learned an important lesson about not angering your dictators. Randy graduated eleventh in his class of more than 300 students at Williamstown High School in 2004. "Don't make enemies of your teachers," he stated emphatically. You see, Randy had a summer reading assignment for his English class prior to his senior year—*Anna Karenina*—a notoriously lengthy novel. He decided to take a different approach to "reading" the book. "I just watched the movie," he said. "And I ended up getting the highest grade in the class on the essay test." Now, life could have been grand with that first impression, but an ill-fated walk down the hallway changed things for him pretty quickly. His previous year's English teacher was seated outside the lavatories on duty, signing students in. Randy had a good rapport with this teacher and talked casually with her about what had happened with the essay test and how he had "studied" for it. "Apparently my senior year English teacher was in the lav and heard all of this," he said, the cringe on his face practically audible. And while he didn't make a true enemy per se, "it wasn't a fun rest of the year. Let's put it that way," he admitted. Rather than focusing on figuring out what his English teacher wanted and expected of her students that year, he had to constantly prove that he was working his butt off and not taking any shortcuts after that. "I had to make sure that I read every book and did every homework assignment," he said.

Now, some teachers you can never please, no matter what you do. Just try your best, and go with it. Nina Lopergolo said that she once had a teacher who just did not like the smart kids, even though he taught a weighted class presumably for students who wanted a challenge. In that case, no "coup" was staged, but the majority won in a different way. "We are diehard. We'll do anything for that grade sometimes," Nina said, describing the top students in her grade. "We're our own species. We're not for everyone. And by the time I had that teacher, we all knew we weren't for everyone. One little point on a test, we'll ask about and sometimes fight you on. And they don't like that sometimes, but we'll do it." And the result with this particular teacher? "We just stayed who we are, and his dislike for us ultimately didn't have that much of an effect because it was like thirty against one. He just kind of gave up on trying to change us."

While you're highlighting various aspects of your personality for different teachers, never fake who you truly are…especially if you haven't won any nationally recognized acting awards recently.

And remember, you might encounter teachers who you have to hide your smarts from more than others, but there are always going to be ones who are proud of your drive and diligence. "I used to be very anxious in school," Nina recalled of her earlier high school years. "My history teacher would come over and hand me a paper clip during tests because I loved to fidget around with it or I'd break my pencils." Now that's an understanding teacher.

Know Your Enemies

Wait, let me try that chapter title again.

Know Your Fellow Classmates

There. Not quite as sinister.

As I already mentioned, I was in a class of overachievers. Fractions of points separated some of us. And so part of winning the game is not only being aware of your teachers, but of the other students in your grade as well.

I could afford to take a non-weighted acting class because all of the kids were doing the same thing. I kept tabs on who was taking a CP class or who was taking that extra AP class. I tried my best to ensure that I was taking at least as many AP classes as "the competition."

After each year of high school, I was able to ask about my current class rank, and I was ranked as the valedictorian after all four years. So for me it was constantly about *staying* ahead and not letting others pass me. By senior year, I had a pretty decent grasp of who the others were in the top ten, and as expected, I was in classes with most of them. And so, as a result of knowing who they were and also me needing to merely stay ahead instead of fighting for position, I was able to make some unusual, strategic choices in group partners my senior year of high school.

Whenever possible, I picked the highest ranked people in my class to be partners with on special class assignments. I did this for three reasons:

1. Generally speaking, these people were kind and like-minded in their work ethic.
2. I knew I wouldn't get stuck with someone who would do no work and dump it all on the "smart kid," knowing that I wouldn't do a bad job so as to not do poorly on the project.
3. If I was getting the same exact grade as the people directly below me, I knew they couldn't get a better grade than me and thus pass me!

Now, I had a unique opportunity to know exactly who was around me in terms of class rank, though usually you can take a pretty good commonsense guess if you don't. My specific knowledge came most unexpectedly during my second year of high school.

Immediately following my freshman year, my guidance counselor had actually called me to excitedly relay that I was on track to be my class's valedictorian. I was ecstatic—I knew that I had been getting good grades, but at that point I still hadn't been sure that actually becoming the valedictorian was attainable since there were hundreds of students in my grade.

And still, as excited as I was, I didn't tell anyone that I was on track to become the valedictorian. A lot can change in three more years, I figured, and I especially didn't want "the competition" knowing that I was the person to beat. Up until that point, I felt I had managed to fly sufficiently under the radar. I was clearly doing well in the top classes, but I didn't have "GENIUS" tattooed to my forehead or anything. At the very least, I didn't think most people would immediately guess that I was number one.

And then I was sitting in the school cafeteria one day during my sophomore year when a friend ran toward me, super excited. "Ellen! Guess what? You're currently the valedictorian!"

My first thought upon hearing this proclaimed to everyone around us? *Crap. There goes my dating life.* But my second thought upon hearing this proclaimed to everyone around us? *Shoot. Now everyone knows I'm the one to beat.*

It turned out that my friend's guidance counselor had showed her the entire class rank list instead of just sharing her personal class rank. She was so excited for me, though, that I couldn't be upset with her for shouting this to the mountaintops. I just happily thanked her for letting me know and hoped that people would forget.

They didn't, and I soon had a bunch of people asking if the rumors were true. I tried laid-back answers, like, "I think so." But it was out there.

My suggestion is to keep your genius a secret. But if it gets out that you're earning exceptional grades, don't flaunt it. For starters, pride goeth before the fall. But also, you're painting a target on your back for, as Nina Lopergolo had put it, the people who "will do anything for that grade."

At least I was able to make one strategic move since my cover was blown, so to speak; I was able to discover from my friend who the other top ten were.

School Musical, Newspaper Clubs, and "Smart People Conferences"

Ultimately, the "game" of school is unique to each individual. You have to be aware of your own limits, personality, strengths, and weaknesses. You have to have a good understanding of how your specific school calculates GPAs, and you need to be aware of your teachers and classmates and *their* limits, personalities, strengths, and weaknesses. But there is another side to being a teenager in high school, and even another part to getting into colleges and setting yourself up for a future career.

Especially when trying to get into a good college, being involved in activities is arguably just as important as good grades.

According to Georgetown University's 2016 "Profile for Schools and Candidates," only 50% of the valedictorians who applied to the university that year were actually granted admission, while only 36% of salutatorians were accepted. So clearly there is more to the college admissions process than pure academics.

As of April 2017, Nina Lopergolo had just recently finished going through the college application and acceptance process. "They don't just want to see the scholar. They want to see how well rounded you are, that you're not one-dimensional," she told me. "They want someone who's going to enhance their community." Nina was accepted to The George Washington University to pursue a degree in biology.

In high school, I was the President of the National Honor Society, had been in several high school drama productions and school musicals, and had earned varsity letters in boys' track to name just a few things I was involved in. (For the record, no, I'm not a boy. But I kept stats for the boys' track team, which, oddly enough, earned me varsity letters. It also added a new dimension to my resume by giving me something sports-related to add, as I didn't have the time to actually participate in a team sport with long practices.)

I was also the editor of our high school's newspaper. This is a perfect example of what I considered a pure resume builder. As an adult, I spoke once to a high school newspaper club since I have a background as a freelance reporter for some large newspapers in my area. This club was full of talent, and their newspaper looked pretty gosh darn close to an actual newspaper. My high school was a bit different than that. While I'm sure there were good writers in my school, the newspaper was just a couple of sheets of paper printed and stapled together and distributed so infrequently I'm not sure that people knew that a school paper actually existed. I never once wrote for it, and was only given the position of editor by my AP English teacher during my last year of high school. She was complaining about how poorly written some of the articles were. (They were mostly opinion pieces as far as I can remember, containing very little actual school news.) She asked if I had any time to help her edit them so that they'd be in decent shape when distributed. I said yes, and used my brief time in homeroom to occasionally edit them, for which I was given the very important title of "Newspaper Editor." Minimal work output and a great sounding title for my resume...I was game. Make sure to follow your passions, but always keep an ear out for these sorts of activities.

Joe Boales didn't bother finding any activities that required a minimal work output. "I was involved in way too many activities," he joked. "I had a part time job that, some weeks, took up thirty to thirty-five hours of my time. I was on the track team for a year, the wrestling team for three years, and academic team, which is basically mathletes, but for all subjects, for one or two years. I was also in the jazz band and the National Honor Society." And while he was a busy student, he found them all to be useful activities. "Most of them were important for meeting friends, and the job was helpful for things like buying my first car, with help from my parents," he admitted. "Track and wrestling helped keep me in shape, which I definitely needed. They also helped me stop thinking for a little while and relax a bit. Jazz band was my favorite thing, though. I got to play cool music, travel, compete with other bands, and hang out with friends. So it had a little bit of everything."

Laura Oliveto actually laughed and exclaimed, "What didn't I do?" when I asked about her extra-curricular activities. "My philosophy was, and still is, an empty mind is the devil's workshop—something my swim coach told me my freshman year, which I took fairly literally. I was a three-sport varsity athlete by my senior year. I played soccer and was on the swim team all four years, and the track team for my last three years. I was an assistant youth soccer coach to my little sister's soccer team. I was a part of the Varsity Club, SAVE club, and I was also a National Honor Society officer. Every single one of these activities was extremely important to me. Playing sports was such amazing stress relief—like I said earlier, I'm a very competitive person, and I like to win. I love playing sports and I had a lot of fun running around, swimming, and hurdling and jumping for my school."

While Joe, Laura, and I were in a wide array of activities, Gina Coyle used her spare time to hone her extra-curricular skills to an impressive level, regarding even these activities as part of "the game." Still, she had a sense of humor about it. "I only did things I was good at," she said, laughing a bit at her strategy. "For example, once I realized I was not a rock star in softball, I stopped doing that."

She was a "rock star" when it came to her singing voice, however. She not only took on lead roles in her school's musicals, but she became a section leader in New Jersey's All South Jersey Choir. She believes that a combination of her class rank and the activities she excelled in helped her to get into college, despite her "underwhelming" SAT score. "I applied to colleges in New Jersey, and my SAT score did not even meet their minimum requirement, and I still got in!" she told me.

Frank Broomell found extra energy to do well academically thanks to his involvement in baseball and then rowing. "Playing sports for me was important because I gained a lot of energy from being involved in team sports. It was a way to get outside, to get active, and it provided energy and motivation to work on classes and do homework and get that stuff done so that I could get to practice and be involved in those things."

Randy Ford participated in one activity that directly impacted his being hired as a legal cleric during his time in law school. Among other activities, Randy had previously participated in scouting for years, eventually as an Eagle Scout. "A lot of the other applicants had better grades than I did, but the man in charge of hiring was an Eagle Scout, and I was an Eagle Scout. Because of that, he told me that he knew I was dependable." Activities that open the door to these types of connections can really be excellent for resumes and job interviews.

Sandy Hogg also participated in a wide array of activities, from sports to the school play. She did participate in one program, though, that really put her leaps and bounds ahead when planning to go to college. She was accepted to and attended the Governor's School for International Studies. Out of the one hundred students chosen to attend, Sandy teased that she was the "one hundredth smartest." She said, "It was actually one of the experiences that shaped the decisions I made going into college." She got the chance to really examine her passions, something I myself spent a year of college and thousands of dollars figuring out. "I saw how passionate everyone else was about international affairs, politics, and diplomacy at Governor's School, and found myself thinking: Oh my gosh. This is so uninteresting to me. I am so glad I'm experiencing this now."

Sandy realized that her love of international studies extended only so far as her love of foreign languages. "My strengths were in subjects that were very systematic," she said, noting how languages are made of parts of speech and rules that govern structure and meaning, like a formula. "Governor's School was a wake-up call and an opportunity to recognize that this is not what I actually like and not what I am actually good at." And so when Sandy went to the University of Maryland, Baltimore County, she studied applied linguistics.

Additionally, this experience helped her plan what type of college she wanted to attend in the first place. "I was kind of miserable and lonely," she said of her time at the four-week Governor's School program. "I felt very stranded and like I had no control," she continued, in reference to the fact that she had no car there and so she literally had no place to go. And so she knew that she needed a place where she could drive around and explore, getting extremely specific with a college's location requirements. "I needed a college that was at least an hour and a half away in order to get the experience of being away from home, but no more than four hours away." Ultimately, she described the college she chose as "perfect."

Whenever you get the opportunity to attend a program tailored to your interests, go and test your interests. That being said, don't be surprised if you change your mind in college or even beyond.

After graduating from high school, I attended The George Washington University's Elliott School of International Affairs to pursue a degree in international studies with a concentration in international politics. After arriving at GW, I found myself literally falling asleep in my international affairs classes out of boredom. As you've hopefully realized through the reading of this book, this was not my usual way in a classroom. And it helped me realize an important thing about myself—I hate politics. And that was really not a good thing to hate when I was supposed to be studying international politics. I quickly remembered something else that I loved, though. In my freshman dormitory, I started writing a story idea I had had in my head since middle school. I started with just a few pages, and I emailed them to my younger sister. She asked for more pages, and before I knew it, I had written my first novel, *Future Vision*. With my love of writing rekindled, I transferred to Rowan University and studied journalism. I quickly became a freelance reporter for The Philadelphia Inquirer, the Courier Post, and many other publications. But after I graduated from Rowan, I decided to try fiction writing full-time. At this point, I've had five novels published: *Future Vision, An Unremarkable Girl, Avenging Her Father, Risking a Life,* and *Blood Moon.*

    I'm not the Secretary of State or a CIA spy like I had planned on when I was in high school, but I'm more than happy with the direction my life has taken.

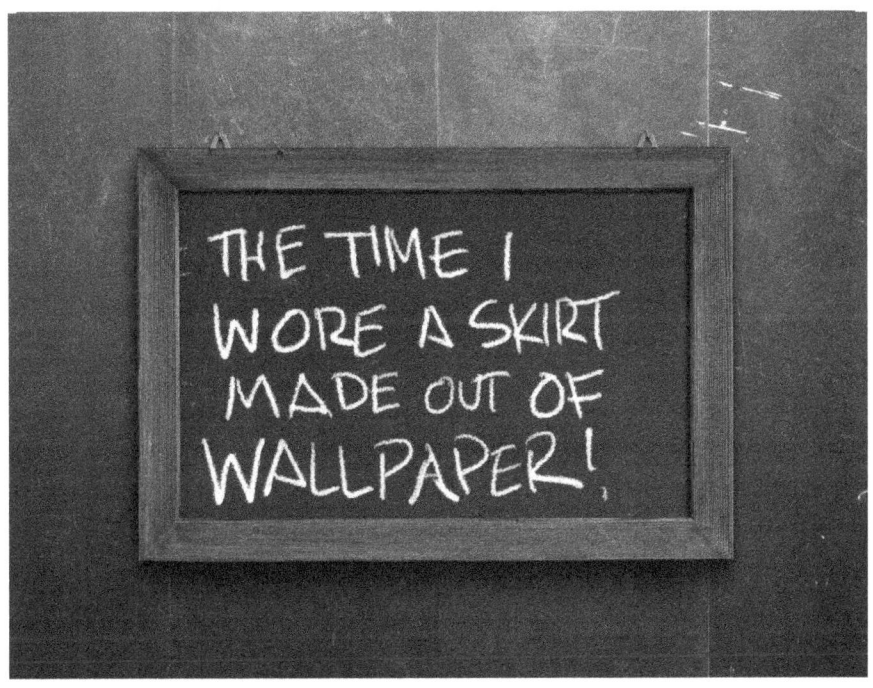

That Time I Wore a Skirt Made Out of Wallpaper

Now for a chapter that might seem to go against everything I have said thus far: There's more to being a high school student than just being a student. Even though I joked about suspecting the death of my dating life after being branded as the smart girl, I had a good social life. Of course it had its ups and downs. Sometimes I was invited to the party. And other times I found myself sitting at a smoothie shop with my friend, Emily, making a pros and cons list of potential guys I was hoping to get to take me to prom since I was unattached.

Being labeled as "the smart kid," can sometimes seem to have an effect, sometimes not. While I had a ton of friends, I didn't tend to date guys from my school, instead branching out to guys from different high schools where my grades weren't the first thing they heard about me. Though for all I know, the guys at my school merely hated the way I said "dude" frequently, or the way I held my pencil in my left hand like a pained robotic claw.

Frank Broomell said that he was labelled as one of the smart kids. "I don't think it impacted my social life negatively. Though I guess you never know what you don't know," he said, laughing. "The smart kids and the good kids probably weren't invited to every party that was going on," he elaborated, "but at the same time, I think my involvement in sports probably balanced out some of the stereotypes that go with that. I was friends with a lot of different cross sections of people at school." He also believed that his school's personality as a small boys' school made it easier to be "the smart kid." He said, "I was lucky to be at a school like St. Augustine where I think a majority of the school looked at academic achievement as something people wanted to do. I think it's what most of the students there are trying to do, which makes it a special environment."

Nina Lopergolo found that her social circle was naturally smaller since she was consistently in difficult classes with the same group of kids. "I think it was fifty kids total who I had connections with out of my whole grade because that's who I was with."

Likewise, I met people for the first time at my high school's Project Graduation on graduation night since I had been with the same group of students in general.

This isn't necessarily a bad thing, though, and can always prevent you from being labeled. Emily DiLorenzo described our own graduating class as follows: I don't really feel like I was labelled "smart" among my peers because basically since middle school we had all been taking honors courses and were in the same classes. So all of us were smart. I only took one college prep course during all of high school—calculus. And that was the only class where I felt like I was the outsider because I was an "honors" kid. But honestly, I had more fun in that class than I did in many of my honors classes because it was so easy for me!

So, in the middle of your crazy, valedictorian-bound life, don't forget to be social. Acquiring crazy, fun stories and friends can certainly help you in the long run with connections and just pure and simple social skills. But honestly, it's got equal, if not greater value, in just being fun!

"Don't be a freak who only focuses on getting good grades. Have fun with your friends too!" my surfer-skater friend, Jessica Mumford, declared in her usual way.

Frank Broomell actually still sees a lot of his friends from high school even though he graduated more than a decade ago. "I left the area for a while between the Marines and graduate school, and last week I went to a party thrown by some friends that I made during high school, and it was as if we had just been hanging out last week."

I once pulled into the parking lot of my school my senior year, took one look at the building, and couldn't bring myself to go inside. So I hopped in a car with two of my friends and we went to Philadelphia for cheesesteaks instead. Another time, I spent all day in a skirt I made out of a piece of floral wallpaper I found in our drama club's prop closet. Gosh, I loved that skirt…too bad it fell apart at the end of the day. (And thankfully I decided to keep my pants on underneath of it.)

Jessica said, "I would go to cross country practice and then we'd go to the beach and the boardwalk and go to someone's house….and then we would just play guitar and be lazy, and it was so much fun." When they were feeling a bit crazy, she and her teammates did different things in Wildwood Crest, New Jersey. "We used to go pool hopping all the time in the hotels until we got kicked out, and that was so much fun." She was laughing as she admitted, "I can still point out all of my favorite pools because I've been in all of them."

Sandy Hogg told me, "I fell into a very tight group of friends later in high school who were a year ahead of me and who I met through the Drama Club. My junior year of high school I started hanging out with them all the time – having sleepovers, doing random things like going to Storybook Land as teenagers, going Christmas caroling, going to the beach after prom, making a slip and slide out of a tarp and dish soap, and just being silly teenagers. Good clean fun. After they graduated, I spent random weekends during my senior year visiting them at their respective colleges and trying to make time for them when they visited home."

A teenage Sandy at Storybook Land,
an amusement park designed especially for young children

My friend, Emily DiLorenzo, once stole her boyfriend's favorite "trucker hat," and the two of us went all around our town, taking pictures of that hat in the most ridiculous places. "We put it on the high school's sign, I posed with it in front of his locker, we took it to his housing development's sign, and we had it at my house posing with fruit," she said, laughing at the silly memories.

And these are just the stories I got permission to retell.

Make sure you allow yourself time to decompress and make your own hysterical memories. But don't put too much pressure on yourself to make your memories top everyone else's! Mark Schoonover told me, "I knew during high school that those four years would certainly not be among the best years of my life, so I wasn't really worried about trying to squeeze every ounce out of the experience. I also firmly believed that a person who considered high school the best years of their life was going to have a pretty miserable go of it after high school was over."

I would tend to agree. So don't put any pressure on yourself while trying to take the pressure off of yourself. In other words, just let yourself have fun and relax. The good times and fun memories will follow.

Where are We Now?

I will never forget standing in front of all of those graduates and giving my valedictorian speech. It was just such a triumphant moment for me. I had tried my best for four straight years, and it had paid off.

Working your butt off in high school can truly help you on the road to incredible things. Though sometimes, as I mentioned in a previous section of this book, those incredible things are completely different from what you had originally planned. And that's okay.

My path to becoming the valedictorian started with simple "try your best" speeches from my parents. I did, and I realized that my best could be something special. God blessed me with intelligence and perseverance, and I enjoyed using those things. As I already mentioned, I also have a legitimate competitive streak in me, and I found a good outlet for that in my quest to become the valedictorian. (I just had to be sure that I remained simply competitive and not destructive. If you find yourself wanting to truly crush the competition, not just metaphorically, then it's probably time to take a step back and reevaluate.) And I also wanted every path open to me when it came time to choose a college and a major. I don't know how many colleges I would have been accepted to. I only applied to The George Washington University and then Rowan University, and was accepted to both.

When I moved into my current neighborhood with my family, we were all excited to meet our new neighbors. I still remember the initial meet and greets:

Me: Hello. Nice to meet you. I'm Ellen Lewis.

A Neighbor: Wait. Ellen Lewis. *The* Ellen Lewis. You—you graduated as the valedictorian from Williamstown High School in 2006! Oh my gosh! I just can't believe I'm meeting you. Can I...I mean, would it be too much to get an autograph?

Okay. That didn't really happen. At all. Not even close. Which actually brings me to an odd, but important point. Your high school achievements will fade as you acquire new adult experiences and successes. And, as I'm sure you are aware, you of course don't need to graduate at the top of your class to become successful:

- My own sister, Alicia Jones, wasn't even close to graduating as one of the top ten people in her high school class, even though she didn't do poorly in high school. "I got mostly A's and B's in high school, but didn't try that hard. Sometimes I did my homework the class before. Imagine if I had actually applied myself!" she said, laughing. She then took a slightly roundabout path through college, starting at Eastern University before going to Camden County and finally settling into the University of Central Florida's Rosen College of Hospitality Management. She's now an event producer for a destination management company and gets to take extended work trips to Hawaii.

Alicia in Hawaii....Clearly, her life is hard.

- Casandra Bowman didn't graduate in her top ten, and there were only fifteen people in her graduating class! Not only that, she just flat-out didn't graduate with her high school class! She went to Gloucester County Christian in Pitman, New Jersey. "I failed history and English, so I walked with my class, but I was the only one who didn't get a diploma that day. I was dead last in my class with the lowest grades and the least favorite student of my teachers. I had more detentions in a month than most students ever have in their lives. I never turned in homework, never studied, and I rarely made it a whole week without skipping a day," she told me. Then, she decided to turn things around. "I graduated nursing school on May 16, 2013—exactly ten years to the day of my high school graduation. When I graduated college, I was president of my class and first vice president of the NJ Student Nurses Association. Now I'm an RN at Capital Health in Trenton, New Jersey. I was chosen to be a unit ambassador for our magnet inspection for re-designation, and I'm currently the chair of our unit council. It may not be a crazy success story, but I went from being the kid that no one thought would ever turn into something, to graduating college and having a successful career."

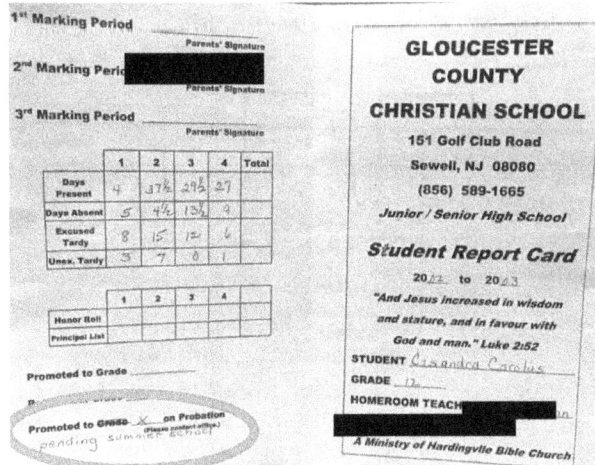
Cassandra's Report Card

Casandra graduating from nursing school.

- Martha Moore also went to a small school, Cumberland Christian School, with a graduating class of about forty people. And while she didn't graduate at the very bottom, she missed graduating in the top ten people. Nevertheless, she went to Rowan University where she graduated in 2009 with a bachelor's degree in American studies with a 3.9 GPA. She then received a Master's of Science in Teaching Elementary

Education from Rowan University in 2010. That time, she received a 4.0 GPA. She taught for five years. During her second year, she started selling her own teaching resources online, which then branched into blogging on myprimaryparadise.com. She became successful through these things, and ended up leaving her teaching position, though she still has a strong passion for education. "I'm able to stay home with my girls *and* reach classrooms all over the world, which is awesome."

Martha Moore and her two beautiful daughters

So, no, you don't have to graduate in the top ten or have a well-rounded resume to be successful. Finishing high in your class potentially *does* make traveling the path you wish to take a bit easier, though. You can get into the colleges you want and start off studying the things you wish to study (even if those things change halfway through college, or halfway through your life).

So how did it work out for the people I mentioned in this book?

- I ended up graduating summa cum laude from Rowan University with a degree in journalism. I already wrote about how I have several novels published, and I love every part of the writing process, from the brainstorming and daydreaming to the editing. In my personal life, I had been dating my husband since almost right after I graduated from high school. We met at church, and he spent my entire freshman year of college taking the train down to Washington D.C. every other weekend to visit me. We married when I turned twenty-one, and we have two kids and two dachshunds, whom we named PB and Jay—the dogs, not the kids. I've truly been very blessed, and the story of my life is still being written.

PB and Jay. Jay is the lazy one in the back,
and PB is the dog in the front with just a hint of her usual crazy eyes.

- After graduating from UMBC, Sandy Hogg stayed close to Baltimore. She currently works at a language services provider in the DC area as a program manager, primarily serving federal clients. She's been happily married since 2014 and currently lives with her wife and dog in Central Maryland.

Sandy (left) with her wife and dog

- My uncle, Dan Rozinski, told me that he wanted to get good grades so that he could get a good job and impress his high school sweetheart, Pam. It must have worked, because Dan and Pam have been married for 33 years now and have had two children. Professionally speaking, Dan went to the University of Pennsylvania where he majored in chemical engineering. He is now a technology fellow for manufacturing and engineering at Dow Chemical—one of the most senior technical positions in Dow and the chemical industry. His focus is on architecting the next generation of technology to enable leading edge digital manufacturing and engineering in Dow plants worldwide. Dan also leads the cyber security strategies and programs across Dow manufacturing and engineering.

Dan looking spiffy and professional

- Gina Coyle currently works as an elementary basic skills teacher. In this role, she is able to teach her students her "work smarter, not harder" philosophy, and she shares all of the tricks she has learned to be successful in school. She has been married to her high school sweetheart, Steve, for eight years. Together they have two intelligent, creative, and adventurous daughters, Savannah and Fiona. When she isn't running around doing the "mom" thing, she enjoys "spending time outdoors with good company and good wine."

Gina and Steve "then." Gina and Steve "now," plus Savannah and Fiona.

- Nina Lopergolo is just starting her post-high school experience, but is excited to be heading off to The George Washington University to major in biology.

Nina posing with GW's unofficial school mascot—a hippo.

- Virginia Parrish double majored in French and education, and double minored in English and psychology during her time at Rutgers University. She taught in public schools for 50,000 years. (Her figure, not mine.) She also worked for Eurolangues, a Paris-based exchange student company, from 1981-1988. She traveled to Morocco several times as a result of working with Moroccan students through Eurolangues. After retiring from teaching, she moved to Fort Worth, Texas. And that's just the basics of how she would describe her life. She is also: "a theater geek from an early age, avid reader from forever, political—way left—junkie from age twelve or so, loyal and enthusiastic Philadelphia Eagles fan, active Methodist, tea drinker, who for many years carried a copy of the US Constitution and the Bible with me on all travels (though I now just refer to them on my phone, but still feel I can't manage without them), Anglophile, historian, antiques aficionado, fluent in French, conversant in Spanish and German, can survive (meaning I can find food and a bathroom) in Italian, Arabic, Japanese."

On the left, Virginia Parrish in high school in 1966. On the right, Virginia Parish today.
(Her response to that picture may have been, "Gah! That hair, though!" But the photo was too cool not to include!)

- Emily DiLorenzo graduated from Eastern University, winning the highest scholarship offered, with a bachelor's in psychology. She worked as a behavioral therapist for children with Autism for nearly two years before moving into a new career in finance and administration. In 2015 she married Drew DiLorenzo. They are both actively involved at their church, Hope Christian Fellowship, with Drew as a drummer and Emily as a vocalist, as well as serving in other ministries. In 2017, Emily made a career change to become an administrative assistant at her church. When Emily isn't at church, you'll find her relaxing at home with Drew and their fruggle puppy, Sirius.

Emily and Sirius looking ADORABLE. (Sirius, that is...I mean, I guess Emily is adorable too.)

- Emily Severance went to Williamstown High School and graduated in 2007 with honors, the English department award, and the New Jersey Stars scholarship. With these in hand, she left to earn her associates degree at Gloucester County College and then went on to Rowan University to earn a bachelor's in English and a bachelor's in secondary education. During her last semester, she was given the Leonard E. Mancuso Medallion Award for Excellence in Student Teaching. After graduating, Emily started teaching English at Millville Memorial High School and stayed for two years. While there, she decided to go back to Rowan University to earn her master's in writing. In 2014, Emily made the move to Timber Creek Regional High School where she is still currently teaching. She married her husband, Ken, on July 4, 2015. During her rare moments of free time from grading and writing, she enjoys trying out new restaurants, seeing a movie, and going to concerts.

Emily and her husband, Ken

- Jessica Mumford is now a full-time mom and part-time banker who spends any spare time outside with her son, Elijah, and husband, Kyle.

Jessica and her son, Elijah, at her favorite place--the beach

- Joe Boales is currently a 27-year-old physics PhD candidate at Boston University. After graduating high school, he went to Drexel University, where he received degrees summa cum laude in physics and mechanical engineering in 2013. While there, he had co-ops at the Princeton Plasma Physics Laboratory, Max Levy Autograph, and the Paulsboro Refining Company. He also had work-study jobs as an office assistant and a peer tutor. After graduating from Drexel, he began his graduate studies in physics at Boston University. For the first few years, he worked as a teaching fellow. During his second year, he received the College of Arts & Sciences Outstanding Teaching Fellow Award then became a teaching fellow peer mentor the following year. Just prior to his second year, he also started working in Dr. Raj Mohanty's lab as a research fellow, where they explore problems ranging from point-of-care detection of cancer to measurements and wireless communication and power using micro- and nano-scale devices. Since beginning in this lab, he has written several papers. One was published in *Physical Review B*, and a second paper is pending publication in *Nature Microsystems & Nanoengineering*.

Joe Boales

- Mark Schoonover attended Eastern University in St. Davids, Pennsylvania. He graduated in three and a half years with a BS in Business Management, and got a job as a warehouse manager. "I told my parents I'd never go to school again," he said. Then he went back to school for engineering in 2012. He currently works as a controls engineer and project manager at Cummins-Wagner. He married his wife, Ann, in 2009 and they have two children.

Mark Schoonover and Family

- Frank Broomell went to The George Washington University where he majored in international affairs on a half scholarship for academics. After he graduated, he served in the Marines for four years active duty. He then went for his master's in public policy at Harvard Kennedy School. While there, he became a Belfer International and Global Affairs Fellow, working with faculty members and staff in their research center. After graduating, he moved to Washington, D.C. where he worked on Capitol Hill as a legislative assistant for a congresswoman, concentrating on veterans, defense, foreign policy, and health care issues. Now he is back in school at the University of Pennsylvania Law School.

Frank Broomell

- Randy Ford went to Rutgers Camden where he majored in Political Science, founding his school's chapter of the College Republicans during his time there. Through Rutgers' dual degree program, Randy started his first year of law school during his senior year of undergrad. He is now an attorney at a law firm in Mantua, New Jersey, with offices in Philadelphia as well. He focuses mostly on software licensing technology. He married in October 2010, and he and his wife have two young sons.

Randy Ford, his wife, Maria, and his sons, RJ and Michael

- Laura Oliveto is a rising junior at Stevens Institute of Technology where she is set to graduate in 2019 with a Bachelor's of Engineering degree in Software Engineering and a minor in computer science. Prior to her senior year, she was an intern in the IT department of a law firm in New York City. She still keeps herself busy and involved at college; she is on the executive board of her sorority, Theta Phi Alpha, a college tour guide, a tutor, an orientation leader, and a student ambassador. She has also been on the Dean's List since her arrival at Stevens Institute of Technology.

Laura Oliveto in front of the New York City skyline

The road to becoming the valedictorian is a long one, filled with trials and triumphs. Embrace your "nerdy" side, and just go for it!

Acknowledgements

As always, I'd first like to acknowledge my Lord and Savior, Jesus Christ. Before I begin writing, I always pray. Because without God, any talent I possess would be nothing.

I'd like to thank Sam Varney from Metal Lunchbox Publishing. He has been absolutely wonderful to work with, and I consider myself very blessed to have such a dedicated publisher.

Thank you, of course, to the men and women whose stories have been told in this book. They are all exceptional individuals; thank you for allowing me to share your insights and experiences. Also, thank you to the people who took the time to talk to me whose words of wisdom were ultimately not included in this book, including Jeff and Ashley; your stories were still inspiring.

My sincere appreciation goes out to the wonderful teachers I had at Williamstown High School. They inspired me, taught me, and even sometimes stood up for me. Also, thank you to the wonderful journalism professors I had at Rowan University. It was nice to get back to my non-fiction roots, and hopefully I make you proud.

Thanks to OTIS for the babysitting so I could write.

While I dedicated this book to them, I'd like to again thank my parents. They were a wonderful source of support and encouragement in my life, and they remain so to this day. Thanks for being there for me during my high school years. And even though I took their "try your best" encouragement more as a challenge than they certainly intended, feeling secure in their unconditional love meant the world to me.

Lastly, thank you to my husband, Al. Not only my unofficial editor in this project, you were also the person with whom I originally shared this idea. You always encourage me to live my dream, and I love you.

ABOUT THE AUTHOR

Ellen Parry Lewis is the author of the young adult novels *Blood Moon*, *Risking a Life*, *Avenging Her Father*, *An Unremarkable Girl*, and *Future Vision*. Before that, Ellen embraced her love of non-fiction as a freelance reporter for several newspapers. She lives in New Jersey with her husband, daughter, son, and two dachshunds.

www.ingramcontent.com/pod-product-compliance
Lightning Source LLC
Chambersburg PA
CBHW031428040426
42444CB00006B/727